The loneliness
of shape

… one of those colossal poets able to bridge worlds—poetry and art, heart and mind—with rare wit, grace, and sincerity; a soft-spoken artist with the courage to face the "fatal beckoning" of his muse … crisp intellect, seamlessly interwoven with loss and longing. … poetry at its best: at once both gritty and refined, private and political, tender and tough as iron … well worth reading."

—Michael Meyerhofer, author of *What to do if you're buried alive*, *Damnatio Memoriae, Blue Collar Eulogies*

…delicately wrought… highly recommended reading…because, ultimately, this witness so clearly loves his subject.

—Eileen Tabios, editor, *Galatea Resurrects*

Riding Thermals to Winter Grounds (2017, Leaky Boot)

… some very powerful lines, such as: "And then, near the end of my life, I become the man I wanted to be without the fuss and bother of giving a damn."

—Sidney Grayling, editor, Onager Editions

કે

Critical praise for Djelloul Marbrook's fiction

Light Piercing Water trilogy (2018, Leaky Boot)

What Marbrook does so well in *Guest Boy* is the contradictory elegance he showed in *Saraceno*. He finds the tender and poetic heart of very tough men. In *Saraceno*, it was low-level mobsters; here it's men of the sea. They're a horny-handed bunch, and Marbrook's familiarity with ships and the characters of mean-street ports is deep and exciting. But Marbrook knows that these guys have a lot more going on within, and are simultaneously deeply tender philosophers. It's a mesmerizing book… You'll find yourself thinking about it long after you've finished reading.

—Dan Baum, author of *Gun Guys* (2013), *Nine Lives* (2009), and others

… a complex work: deep, passionate, exciting and beautifully written with flashbacks and imagery merging real and surreal.

—Sanford Fraser, author of *Tourist* and *Among Strangers I've Known All My Life*

… it is in books like this that I seek answers and guidance as I travel my own path to enlightenment and contentment. This book opened a struggle in me…

—Isla McKetta, editor, *A Geography of Reading*

Artemisia's Wolf (title story, *A Warding Circle*, 2017, Leaky Boot)

...Djelloul Marbrook's impressive novella...successfully blends humor and satire (and perhaps even a touch of magic realism) into its short length...an engrossing story, but what might strike the reader most throughout the book is its infusion of breathtaking poetry...a stunning rebuke to notoriously misogynist subcultures like the New York art scene, showing us just how hard it is for a young woman to be judged on her creative talent alone.

—Tommy Zurhellen, *Hudson River Valley Review*

...lets his powerful imagination run wild, leading the fiction into unexpected corners where weird performers hold court and produce endings that both astonish and are frequently magical.

—James Polk, *The Country and Abroad*, former contributing editor of *Art/World*.

Saraceno

Djelloul Marbrook writes dialogue that not only entertains with an intoxicating clickety-clack, but also packs a truth about low-life mob culture "The Sopranos" only hints at. You can practically smell the anisette and filling-station coffee.

—Dan Baum, author of *Gun Guys* (2013), *Nine Lives: Mystery, Magic, Death and Life in New Orleans* (2009), and others

...a good ear for crackling dialogue... I love Marbrook's crude, raw music of the streets. The notes are authentic and on target...

—Sam Coale, *The Providence* (RI) *Journal*

... an entirely new variety of gangster tale ... a Mafia story sculpted with the most refined of sensibilities from the clay of high art and philosophy . .. the kind of writer I take real pleasure in discovering ...a mature artist whose rich body of work is finally coming to light.

—Brent Robison, editor, *Prima Materia*

Alice Miller's Room
(title story, *Making Room*, 2017, Leaky Boot)

This enchanting novella is a delicately wrought homage to Jung's famous principle of meaningful coincidence...

—*Breakfast All Day*, UK

... the story draws us into that mysterious and terrifying realm where the heart will have its say and all who enter leave transformed...

—Dr. Patricia L. Divine, Head Start program lifetime service award winner

Mean Bastards Making Nice (2014, Leaky Boot)

I love it. I admire it. It is you at your best.

—Novelist Gail Godwin on "The Pain of Wearing Our Faces"

The loneliness of shape

poems by

Djelloul Marbrook

LEAKY BOOT PRESS

The loneliness of shape
by Djelloul Marbrook

Acknowledgments

"Skullduggery" and "Paying the plumber resentfully" appeared in the May-June 2017 issue of *La Presa*, the Embajadoro Press Journal.

These poems were inspired by readings about quantum physics, such as George Musser's renowned *Spooky Action at a Distance*.

First published in 2019 by
Leaky Boot Press
http://www.leakyboot.com

ISBN: 978-1-909849-70-9

Author's Acknowledgments

Endless thanks are owed to my wife, Marilyn, who has in so many ways made all my work possible; to James Goddard, my publisher, whose steadfast faith in my work brought it to light and buoyed me in rough waters; to Sebastien Doubinsky, who published my work and introduced me to James Goddard; to Brent Robison, whose wizardly videos and deft hand with e-books still astonish me; to Kevin Swanwick, whose radiance as a reader and advisor unfailingly enlightens me; and to Emily Brooks, whose artistic taste, good cheer and resourcefulness seem fathomless.

for my beloved wife Marilyn

Prologue

*We are all facets
of the same jewel.*

Contents

Proem

Entanglements

People

Shape

Place

Shadowtime

Capitalism celebrates the individualist but spends fortunes trying to turn the individualist into consumer-bot. These poems confront that paradox head-on. They're about our oneness, our indivisibility. They speak of our names, our stereotypes, our categories as baggage that hinders our understanding of ourselves as part of a cosmic whole, a whole that could be described as Giordano Bruno's triumphant beast. These poems are inspired by readings about quantum physics, such as George Musser's renowned *Spooky Action at a Distance*.

The loneliness of shape is about the baggage we have been forced to carry through life to prevent us from taking flight, from seeing each other as essential to the symphony of the stars. These poems speak to objects and matters so ordinary we are likely to ignore them—the movement of curtains in windows, the odor of old rooms, nails backing out of rotting wood, a glance in the street. *The loneliness of shape* is a moment's relief from the great burdens imposed on us by the ordering of society to serve the few. These poems challenge the way we are parsed by marketers in order to be sold goods, services and ideas and the way we are coerced into thinking of ourselves. They explore our connectedness, our action on each other, our operation as elixirs, our oneness, our indivisibility.

—*DM.*

Proem

Assignation

Earth, urn and motherboard contain
droplets of the tryst
in which tomorrows swim
to farther shores.
All that can be poured into something else
is nothing compared to the crack in the zero
by that assignation's humming reaching us.
We live and drown in their rapture,
occasionally not resenting it.

Sham, our names and shapes, composed
to trick us into containment.
Obsessed by vessels we suppose,
we can sell our priceless essences
in the shadows of our cathedrals.
But we can't, we can only delude ourselves
with yet another civilization.
All we say we are we're not
no matter what we put in bottles
or how we label them.
We are instead the grand impulse
to become something more
and from that more to wrest
the wrongful taxes of delusion.

Entanglements

World without edge

If nothing's as we think it is
and we suppose for convenience's sake
there's a here and there distinct
from a world without an edge
not only are all bets off
but we're free to own our imaginings
and admit we know more about each other
than we've ever dared cop to more
in fact about entanglements
than is safe for comfort which in any case
is as overrated as being right.

One

I'm to society as a poncho to rain, a vampire to light,
playing my role in our entanglements poorly,
not an individualist but a maniac
shedding a quantum of light
not so much damages as salvages.

I'm allergic to the nuances of matrices
and would settle for being rogue if I had the wit,
but as it is I must dance my way through the drops,
sidling, charming, offending, frightened and frightening,
bedeviled by gnats that are either memories or happenings
somewhere else, somewhere sending signals
as if I were a homing device.

I'm acoustically impaired to misconstrue
whatever arrives however long it took
and in this scrambling I derive not pleasure
but the algebra of a dervish whirling
in the entanglements I find hospitable.

Graviton to graviton, sub-atom to sub-atom,
letter to word, word to poem,
I'm essential to the one
that runs in rivulets off my back—
essential is my will to rebel,
otherwise I would not trouble you with this.

Bone conductivity

My skull is a cement violin
hijacking sounds en route to my brain.

The bow saws in vain as I wait
for meaning to arrive,
staring out of two bullseyes
at the swamps of Gehenna.

When meaning is decoded
I dissect it like a medical examiner.

What's new about this diagnosis?
Meaning has never come in time.

I've always had to wing
my native language in lonely bus stops,
waiting for words to fail
or to be arrested on suspicion
of being someone else, someone
wanted more than me.

My papers have never been in order.
The driver might as well be a cop,
nor is my skull resonant enough
to marry sounds to meaning,
and so I understand jazz
and tell when it comes to trumpets
Telemann from Mozart and Purcell,
but when you ask me a question
or give me an instruction
I can't hear you for the rain
or see you through the blur of my anxieties.

Randomness to dissuade

Is the universe itself a being
and we its creaturely parts,
therefore essential to each other
in spite of our mythologies?
I ask the question in defiance
not of common knowledge
but supposing I'm a molecule of the beast
assisting in some reaction.
Is that not to say I have come home
from the illusion of unbelonging,
not as grand as being a pore of the beast,
a black hole, but grand enough
considering all the pomposities I've had to pop
as a cigarette pops balloons?

I'll never forget this special I can't remember when
but occasionally the sea gives it up
like a sunken ship and then
the right thing happens at the wrong time,
the wrong thing happens at the right time
to litter streets with butts.
Is it because we're holograms
who have annoyed the beast
or beloved friends shown the way?
Or beloved friends shown away?
What trail do I follow in fear,
what iron tricks the compass?
Does the dappling sun camouflage intent,
directing me to my next mistake?

In this surgical mathematics
I'd welcome a discarded condom
to turn my thoughts to defiance
and perhaps a moment's ecstasy
even if it were not mine,
a randomness to dissuade
buzzing paranoia.

All that brains itself against my eyes

Born wrong, don't give a damn about being right,
light changes, clouds move on, winds sweep out my mind,
and all that brains itself against my eyes
makes someone's spring fertile.
I care about this, no matter how casual I sound,
going easy on the melodrama so as not to fall all over myself,
trying to get over myself, failing by the very act—
what the hell, who's that there whose smirk is more genetic
than commentary on what I'm doing here?
I never know what I'm doing here, reading faces to find out,
finding out more than I can handle, never know,
never pretended to know, if I may say a good thing of me.
My face eats through my other masks to bare the bone of
dismay—
acid, penetrant, but not penitent, I've never had the stuff
to describe the meaning of the elements.

The next what-have-you

Just as I am used to being old
the next what-have-you is death
with all its possible variations.
I never rose to the usual occasions
—birth love marriage sex—
but I used my antennae well
and they did me mercilessly
as if to stay in shape.
I thought death might be a punishment
for not respecting them,
and so this life as a flagellant
has had to be disguised in words
so as not to speak the unutterable one.
Our names are as inappropriate as we are
to the situations in which we find ourselves.
Our grandeur is in how we improvise.

Not a shopper fingering

I want to be a hurricane,
not a shopper fingering a rack of pronouns,
finding they don't fit.
I want to trundle the Ferris wheels of Jersey,
pluck Manhattan's harp.
I want to tune Long Island's fork,
hook fingers with Cape Cod,
lollygag at sea as if
I'd been an innocent at play.
I want to drive salesgirls mad,
mad enough to get a life.
I want to drown the weatherman
who tried to cage me with a name.
I want to churn ghost ships in Hatteras mists,
toss them up on Ocracoke,
I want to be the verge of speech.

Leaves

Now with gasoline to-do
we blow the leaves to heaps
and suck them up because
all that exists is made of ruin.
But we don't do it reverently enough
because all that others know
is subject to our denial.
It's hard to know what to do or not to do
or how much ado to make of it,
but if we account for stars and they for us
we should reconsider the uses of despair,
and study the design of leaves
as if they are our ancestors,
considering them more dutiful than ourselves.
And when it comes to lords and masters
how can we be certain who're the slaves?
In ignorance breathes the only hope there is,
but first we have to cajole infinity
to welcome it.

Corrections

Time jumped back just enough to say
schedule is false proof
we're where we should be
and no such thing as given time
obeys us but is in abeyance
and this suspense nurtures us
while the corrections we rely on
deflect us from adventure.
Did I gain half an hour or
did the glamors of the night
lure me from the charms of this oasis?
I know I'm made of stars operating
in my genes, and so the seconds
and hours—they don't pass for me.

Death & possession

Possession is our curse—
the ravishing athlete,
the shining Maserati,
all that we are dying to own.

All that belongs is a death cult,
all who belong its celebrants.
We are either one, one and another,
or we are cancer cells.

Solace

Calm settles on my leaves.
Motionless.
I look everyone in the eye.
I exude the perfume
of wanting less at last,

not in the eye of a hurricane,
its whipping tail to come,
but in unhurried dispensation
from the summons of bright objects
and the allure of grand ideas.

Drought

Thunderstorms piddle, earth thirsts,
politicians drivel. I shop for a stopper
to stop a carafe, aware
that 15 years ago the towers fell
but sick of flag-wrapping greed
I am looking for a cork,
a certain circumference,
to celebrate concerns
Alexander wouldn't have troubled
his hoplites with, hoping
to believe it is as much news
of our society as Donald Trump.
For all I know it might even bring rain.
After a lifetime of editing news
I think half-burying this jug
of blue sea glass in an old stream bed will do
more good than the next election,
but among a race of quantifiers
my thoughts brace themselves against
the pure damned hatred of mystery.

Rooted in the wind

I have been ruthless in my rootlessness
partly because I hate pretense
mostly because I do not trust the earth,
earth that bestiary that shook my crib,
stalked me in the hall, startled me at the sink,
what have my tendrils to do with it?
Was trust possible?
If not the question was
how soon to dry up and blow away.
I am rooted in the wind.
I have dragged my anchor across the specific,
a ghost ship peopled by the lies I have lived.
I am trying fervently to understand
why I could not reach around the rocks
to the find the lambent lap of clay.

Loitering

So if we're dying from each moment on,
putting off and putting on, is loitering
a kind of panic attack of not getting on,
are gravestones and accomplishments debris,
acknowledgments that we failed
to drop identity and proceed unhinged
to any door or gate, proof
against being contained, a certain fragrance,
peculiar to each skin, vitally unconcerned
with heritage and legacy, A to Z
rolling zero like a hoop down the street,
a child collecting memories, innocent
of intent? Loiter 's not to linger,
nor exactly to make a nuisance of oneself,
but I think it is to litter the studios of artists
with our pretensions and complaints,
and no stop-and-frisk policy deters the litterer
from spoiling what the artist paints.

At that moment

Not because we can't have
but because we don't know what having means.
I have what I see but what I want is to kill.
Will it be light or dark enough
to see you when I give up my name?
Giving up my name, will I find such questions tedious
and at that moment recall how many times I've seen you,
astonished and understanding astonishment?
Is that all I was called upon to live?
I don't know, I wish I knew how to testify.

Giantesses

What if I were sea glass or heron-still,
tide-worn to gem unmindful
of having to think of anything?
Would I then serve the purposes of this womb
in which we presume to have been born?
Would angels gather around me,
would I welcome being born,
would I trade my questions
to be an emerald and be worn by
giantesses in whom black holes are pores?

Bleeding out

I could say I remember this and that
or I could walk on by—
bite of wind, pelt of leaf,
poor excuses not to speak
and yet we grasp them,
being made of inopportunity,
and in fear of blowing away
hunch our shoulders and look the other way.
You see someone else in back of me,
I fear the cards are marked, and between us
we bleed out synchronicity.

Glaciology

The future is walking back on me,
not giving an inch away,
and even if I sidestep or pretend
interest in a shop window
it comes on with the same velocity
that everything else hits me,
so I walk backwards apace,
visiting vaults and instances
frozen in the crevasses of my brain,
talking to the perfectly preserved,
examining artifacts and lost occasions
as if someone's life depends on it—
my own is forfeit
to what I'll tell you in another poem,
maybe, and if not you'll have this newfangled pick
to break the ice.

'Spooky action at a distance'
—*Albert Einstein*

Because you pretend not to see me
doesn't mean I must step aside
nor that my wont not to be in the way
should license your entitlement.
You're not a rush of events to filter
but one who made an instant decision
to seize a neutral space
for the country of your ego.
I see too much that's hidden
without any special lens,
my mind is not a photoshop,
it's a stormy cucurbit
where terrible elixirs operate
on the species I've let in—
their dreams, memories and imaginings
to which I'm kindling, content and constituent.
You and your three-abreast scorn
shoulder this age-spayed critter
at your peril should this taken note
spook the distance between object and instance
Einstein talked about.

People

Anchors

Torn away,
unwelcome anywhere, unmoored, unhitched, unhinged.
Gone the Breyer's ice cream cart,
gone Peggy swinging me out over the ocean,
gone the mushroom anchor buried in affection,
gone the Danforth plowed into understanding,
gone the fisherman's anchor diddling the tumblers of the sea.
If they were not illusions, not holograms,
if they did not need names,
how do I respect them in my old age?
Surely to die in disrespect,
to have been nothing more than a vandal,
would be to flatter the walleye of unwelcoming ones.
Not that I don't the trust the current
or the wind-sculpting sun,
but that my keel bone is tired,
my cargo betrayed, my strakes divorced
from the ambitions of the charts,
charts soaked and stained
with memories spilled by my trembling hand.
Without an anchor I'm not my phony self,
but young again, weather's child and dangerous.

Aurora

The few people who are glad to see him
are misguided fools or fellow daemons,
and in any case they grasp a thrashing cable
not for some greater good
but simply because they could.
He knows this, which explains why he so often
crosses the street to avoid them.
The storm that loosened him was mild
compared to the ones he seemed to have withstood.
So it is with trees and power lines.
He is something you do in private,
a bowel movement, an orgasm, a heart attack
in the light of a super-moon,
an instrumental inconvenience
not a handshake at a coffee hour
nor a conspiratorial wink
but the calamity to which you've been looking forward,
or is it the calamity to whom you've been looking forward,
even though you look the other way?
He is not your Victor Frankenstein
or even the lightning needed,
but he is that aurora at the end of town,
and you are about to become a missing person.

Lucas Cranach's breakfast

The waitress puzzles over Lucas Cranach
sitting in the corner booth,
having sat for him five centuries ago.
Outside a Harley gunning warns
her not to indulge the big ideas
swelling under her blue uniform.
Lucas studies her hands to see
what she has been doing since
he made her scented bosom famous.
Satisfied, he speaks a language
she remembers, but its meaning
meanders before it reaches her brain.
Is this the end of everything
and the start of something else
to which the Harley and its now
inconsequential rider are opposed
or will Lucas once again betray her
to the ordinary? I am his fetch,
she thinks improbably. How
do I know this word? Fetch—
did I cop it from the Khan Academy?
Must I bring him his bill?
We owe each other so much.
I'm immortal. I, I know what—
I'll just stand here and stare at him,
and then, then will he be able
to turn me over to his son?

Certain people walking

To walk elegantly yet not call attention to oneself
is as rare as a fairy sighting.
It's the way a well-found ship cuts through the water
not arguing with it but parting a lover's hair.
Sometimes it's seemed to me my life depends
on witnessing this profane act
not as voyeur but idolator,
a pagan on the cusp of Christianity.
I've been on the lookout for it
as if I'd been born a choreographer.

Elaine

Why do I put the car where it couldn't've been
instead of where it was when I remember Elaine McMahon?
Is this a conundrum Einstein or Bohr would've liked
or would it have spooked them as it spooks me
because now I think everything hangs on answering it?

I know how angry Carol Lonsbury was to see
Elaine become entangled in my eyes, but Carol
is standing behind me in the right place, an ember
charring as if I must rush forward to where
Elaine couldn't be or risk some kind of purgatory.

Silly, isn't it, a childhood incident stuck
in space time, haunting me for no particular reason?
—except that we went on to live different lives
than we imagined that summer when it seemed
we could move the universe around and be
anything, anyone we wanted to be,
gods and goddesses, keys to hidden mysteries.

A doctor retires

I thought we were going to be friends.
You never know. Circumstances crumble
and something far too bright emerges in the ruins,
so bright and sharp the ivy cannot cover over it.
And so he walks down to the lake,
careful of the rattlesnakes,
and stares into the turbid past
hoping less for clarity than surcease.

A go at figuring it out

I don't know what to say to you,
you're never where I put you,
I've run out of fixatives.
My left-handedness has caught up with me
signifying sinister bastardy,
and you act as if you always knew it,
knew at some point my true self would emerge
and you wouldn't have to shit on my grave
just to prove it. We've got each other's number,
so we don't have to go out to lunch
and argue over the tab, making faces
other people can hear, or even bother
to hold the waitress's attention,
because we're cool, we're good, no problem,
and all that's left to decide is which one of us
attracts flies and makes that guy over there mad.

He pulled it off

This is an eyewitness account.
He went into that restroom and never came out.
I thought I'd pee in my shoes,
but I became distracted by his whereabouts.
I searched the cabinets and the floor
for a trapdoor. I attributed my confusion
to old age, but the notion dogged me
I'd seen a dervish disappear.
Arguments are never about truth.
Truth is in the cracks. I swear he went in
and never came out, and I'm satisfied
that should be my epitaph. Never mind my name,
it's not my credibility. He pulled it off.
Better you not believe.

Every palliative its harm

If our lives were staged and choreographed by the Bolshoi
would we tire of beauty and quickly seek the solace of war?
Would we clap in unison or let the critics tell us how to live?
Does every palliative do its harm,
every solution need its Putin, every society its Pentagon?
What's this about evolution if not to hold hands
and leave the theater whole?
If I had answers I'd be at least a Balanchine,
my mind Nijinsky, my costumes sewn with golden thread,
but if the quest in question means anything
I might just be reborn a lighting director.

Frenzy

Black-eyed Susan hoists the heat dome
to her golden shoulders.
Spent peonies shudder in her shadow,
a fawn dies in macadam sweat,
a hawk stoops on the pond—
all is well in the body politic
but what is well
for us who work to make things right,
trying not to get run over or gotten over on,
can we cut off the fuel supply
of those who vacation on our fears
or at least jack up the prices?
Black-eyed Susan doesn't care,
she has taken care of all of it
while we frenzy at Walmart,
chokeweed that we are.

Tinkling underwater

He stands on one foot like a crane
to put on a balky sock.
Your breath could send him
scuttling down the street
in paper shreds but you refrain
for the sake of the children
you might have had
if you both had not been obsessed
with that hole in the wall
in which you saw other lives unraveling.
You wondered what a crash he'd make.
Would it have been more like crystal
tinkling underwater?
Would you have been enthralled to see
he'd never been more than a way
to study the grain of a wooden floor?
Now he's putting on the other sock.
Could he have stood there all night
occasionally falling into the tide
of pebbly dreams?
Draw a deep breath and consider
what a merciful god you are
standing barefoot in your nightie
desperate and calm.

Down at the Big Deep

Did the waitress and the lineman marry
and have a life as exquisite as their tryst
at the swimming hole? Did she remember
blowing a kiss at the boy she hadn't noticed until...
did the lineman remember waving
as if nothing could go wrong with the world?
And could they have possibly guessed
that for a moment they were gods
and the boy would always apologize
for having been there and yet be unable
to imagine life had he not?

If he wasn't Balzac or Rodin

Perhaps he looks like the Balzac nude by Rodin,
pedestal for balls, but I think of him as the exhibitionist
who did me wrong, wrong at such an early age
I have been able to pretend it happened to a friend of mine.
If he wasn't Balzac or Rodin, or even pot-bellied, then
who was it covered my mouth with his hand
and winked at me across the breakfast table?
And where are all those people now
who really weren't there when
the little boy didn't know how to bleed?
I don't wish they've gone to hell,
but should I, can I wish them well?
It's just about being you, a body of water—
not tomorrow, not then—illusorily contained.
It's about the wonts of your ghost ships,
the tears that filled your navel,
the storms that prowled sea routes,
the shifting positions of your body that caused catastrophes
while we're praying for salvation in church
and drowning in someone else's ecstasy and grief.

Never mind

What is this acting as if to alight
only to flit away? Something seen in Madame Butterfly
or something learned in the crib in order never to admit
anyone to a holy of holies you're not sure of yourself?
What is this exquisite extension
withdrawn when you ought to have followed it
into the realm of other, into the arms
of mad Nijinsky and the utter chaos
upon which art depends? I know, I know,
you don't understand a word of this
and other such stock disclaimers and caveats
as to assure the mediocrity you were born to destroy.
That is your tragedy, mine is to witness it.
Never mind who you are, any you will do,
any me will do, the point is that we see
more than any shrink will ever extract from us
and retain it to make ourselves interesting.

Skullduggery

My skull is a homing device
and when flesh will have fallen away
a priceless relic.
I hear your lurking submarines and signals
of unimaginable creatures.
Accordingly, my behavior would have you think I'm deaf
if only to pretend we're not who we are
nor do what we do.
Baritone brothers sing from a choir loft
over my right eye,
sisters sing behind a rood screen
in the corner of my left eye.
Spheres play across the horizon of my skull
and color an aurora of epiphanies.
All this directionality is not to be laid to rest
but to be an eternal instrument
even when it's dust
and as dust particulates of gods.
My skull knows where the oboes are,
the cellos and the trumpets,
it distinguishes your murmurings
from the politics of frenzied news
and sometimes holds your Delphic yearnings
in reverence and awe as if it might exist for them
and even when it forgets who you are
it remains nostalgic.

Vulgar possession

I

I'm not like that,
yoking a woman with supposed affection
in the public street,
terrified of loss
as if vulgar possession
is anything but illusion.
I'm too wicked for that,
even as a little boy,
the acrid pretense
of well-wishers
spoiled me for society.
This one thing the ruined boy knew,
this unholy thing:
to covet is to kill,
and so we must let be
in adoration scented with sorrow.
How did the ruined boy know?
By his resolve, I think, to be unlike
invaders wearing familial faces
or victims of the the Holocaust
in which our children are Jews
or gypsies to be experimented on.
He wouldn't be an experiment,
knowing as he knew when to leave.
But there are only so many somewheres to go,
and so he happens to walk behind
them as she turns and he notices
she's not as possessed as her possessor thinks.

II

I see with a wicked eye,
wicked in its love
of lifting up the skirts
of settled matters
and redefining them in ways
that incite history to riot.

Hello, little do you know
I've just written a poem about you
in an effort to free you of your thingyness,
or do you know,
know in some way
that scatters words like egrets
standing on a water chestnut isle
as insubstantial as belief?

Marvelous-looking people

Marvelous-looking people spill all over the table
towards me invasively. Bring the bar rag quickly.
But it's always too late, and my wet lap
must dry in the street. Spill over, loud looks,
whatever distracts you from yourself,
spill over on me, quench my arid fields,
don't drown my villages or gully
my switchbacks to insight, don't percolate
in my abasements. Replenish my reservoirs.
Don't cross the table teeming with cheap exports.
The tin ceiling with its bad acoustics
is as merciless as your property rites.
You tie-dye and batik me with your overruns.

Imagine him

His face comes off in his hands.
He sleeps holding it as he dreams another one
and in the morning he pretends
he had none and all are free
to imagine him a suitable someone,
a demon or a daemon, and he
has only to watch from behind his head
as a photographer would
or a child behind a tree.
It would be a frightening affair
were it not an ablution,
and free of having to look a certain way
he could honestly say how do you do
in the full intent of inquiry.

Six on the Beaufort

In such a face mournfulness is hard to explain.
She is a destroyer making flank speed
through number six on the Beaufort Scale.
Her puzzlers are jetsam in her wake
as if they had been the cause of that daunting stare.
I would give a precious certitude or two
to tell her, You have moved me, but the light changes
and I am in someone else's way.

Ahab

Who do the four-legged fail?
Do they bear a grudge,
the dolphin and the whale?
Is Ahab father of us all?
Are we impaled to what we hunt?
Are they haunted, dreams
disturbing those betrayed?
I don't expect answers, I set
the questions like paving stones,
and when they're wet with tears
I know I may slip and fall,
not for asking but for daring
to follow my feet into the dark.

Coquito sky

On this rock Courtney Rodney sat studying stars,
slugging moonshine out of Mason jars. The dairy farm
behind him is now a glassy dental emporium.
He'd been a circus acrobat, the boy a summer wraith
into whose head he poured so much of his life
he hardly needed the residue, so with one last swig
he joined the snow devils that winter, and a stop sign grew
where he'd sat. The boy is older now than Courtney was
and a coquito sky obscures the stars.

Worrying

Worrying about the wrong thing
is to shilly-shally when
alarm bells ring and a skinny woman walks
with two chairs slung over her shoulders
down a street whose name
your dreams are devoted to erasing.
The best of enigmas are not to solve but savor,
which is the harder thing to do
and explains all this dithering.
Even jubilation comes of it,
this alleluia of savoring,
but that requires trust in what and who,
and that may be as humble as sea glass
and dragonflies.

Campari & Tabasco

So, these friends of yours with marvelous friends,
do they occasionally come in boats
to see you slap the ocean with your tail
and spout as if your life depended on it?
Do they piss on you in lit-up gardens
when they've had too much to drink?
Do they snarl at the mention of you?
Don't answer, I'd rather slurp Duxbury oysters
and drown your friends in Tabasco sauce.
I'd rather sip Campari than worry
about a school of mackerel
about to be swallowed by a whale.

Shape

The loneliness of shape

Each image yearns to cross over
to that other being to become
more completely what it is,
but to do so it needs us
not to stand in its way,
and yet the whole of our society
is a barrier against
the barbarity of its will.

Hollow bones must resonate
with an image's melancholy
to sing a crystal bridge
from one to another and so
to leave oneself behind
for the sake of a glimpse
of rites too sacred to see—
and the bridge must reverberate

with yen not yet beaten out of us
for something seen at dusk,
something rods and cones draw
when it stops to study us
and then is gone as we set out
to make a poem or a painting
in the loneliness of shape
and the bitterness of name.

Drawing

Now, vertical lines, you can depend on them,
but horizontals are a matter of opinion.
Perspective begins with you, but someone
is standing in back of you, a kind of sun
for whom you're the shadow, and your job
is to get out of the way, and if that's too eerie
perhaps you ought to take a photograph.
There's no getting the horizontals right
or wrong, but an Apollonian would
not agree with a Dionysian about it,
and there's no coloring your decision—
horizontals are where you say they are and you
will have to live with that, as Vuillard did,
and if Mondrian interrupts your dream
start all over again as if there's no horizon
and everything moves away from you
to the pupil of an infinite eye. Laugh,
put your pencil and your charcoal down,
count to four, exhale, and consent to be drawn.

Doctor's beast

Curious, not thirsty, I sipped tulip dew
and became a tethered creature,
a doctor's beast, no longer streaming.
I wore lead shoes and pushed against the world.
I had no word for it, but I felt anger.
The priest moved on. Others waited
to give up being immaterial.
Burdened with words, I could not warn them.
Harnessed to a name, I hauled
the understandings of tottering men
from one pile to another, exuding
not the usual harmonies but foul humors
and excrescences that humiliated me.
Having offered such a cup, a priest
would move on, and I who worshipped everything
became an iconoclast, my dread soma
a mace flailing at the prisoners
who once I longed to touch and love.
At dusk I would have drifted away,
but it was morning, a bell was ringing,
and I guess I wanted to be summoned,
so long having been a summoner. I looked
for a new kind of drunkenness
and found it in containment and grief.

Black Twig apple

The star of an apple has five points.
Here's what I make of this, it's more reassuring
than anything about me,
but if appreciation depends on dissecting it
and eating won't reveal it, heroism must be
in giving it away, or would that be
a form of cowardice? I can't say,
but I think it worth mentioning
it's a kind of pentagram that with five vertices
makes a golden ratio that ought to be considered
before throwing the core away.
You understand all this, this wasteful meditation,
is a divertissement to distract you from
your grueling dreams which if they tasted
like the Black Twig apple would
be remembered in the morning.

Without our gewgaws

How did the Victorians sit without resort to our gewgaws?
Were they still in the lap of hullaballoo?
Did class somehow reprieve them from having to engage
as our doodads rescue us
from awkward silences and walleyed glances?
They learned how to draw. That means they studied faces,
the geometries of objects and the shadows they cast.
I'm assaulted by these questions in a noisy bistro
as if they were not my own.

What if I had been a mannequin?

What if I *have* been a mannequin?
What then will I have briefly seen,
a predator who lost his taste for meat?
What digestion did I wear?
Was it fashionable?
Who touched me inappropriately
knowing I would be unmoved?
I was expected to be moved,
but on occasion passersby
noticed being noticed
and might have even seen me smile
or register a tic.
That's the way it is with us children left for dead.
You'd better dress us up who knew us naked well
and when they raise the rent and you move on
you'd better not leave us in the dumpster
for some poor artist to find
and paint our testament.

Café

Camera, cup, pot of tea,
a ballet of objects
moving imperceptibly,
pretending to be still
not for our sakes,
we are incidental,
but for what is yet to be
when glaciers melt
and oceans rise
and objects take the camera's picture.

Afterimage

Her afterimage chars the edges of what I want to see
until it curls around a vanishing point in which we disappear.
Who sat in this room by this now still fireplace?
How has this décor dealt with them,
these sinister irises, this burgundy camouflage?
Not well, I think, or I would not be wondering.
I don't know what I'm doing here.
The stated purpose is massage.
Here is always an ambiguous place.
I hear a woman speaking. Is it to me? It's English,
but I don't understand, except that it's urgent
and is probably why I'm here, a situation similar
to having been born, and so this mahogany's inevitable,
these recessed lamps as inappropriate
as I've always been, as here, any here, has been
to my alien eyes. What does she want of me,
with whom is she sitting by this fireside,
what can I glean of this room, now a spa,
that might make the next moment habitable
so that finally I could say I know what I'm doing here?
I know, I know, self must subside,
let roses in the backyard bloom, sun barge through the door,
the woman speak.
Subside, so that all that's deranged is sound advice
and finally her words reach my brain intact.

Paying the plumber resentfully

I grew up a sink for attractants to wash their hands,
my mind a trap for runoff and debris,
my corroded faucets and cracked porcelain
a certain kind of modernism
that celebrates but does not revere distress.
Plumbers fixed me from time to time.
I paid them resentfully.
Those who've washed their hands of me
assumed approval in my gurgle.
Piped into hell, my face turns up to heaven
in case its delegates should appear.
I could have said I'm a toilet
but would that have conjured Pilate
and his absolution of an empire?
In every child of whom we wash our hands
we do this in remembrance of him
and call it all sorts of high-sounding names
when it's nothing but another of our games.

Studying to be a fool

My most exquisite failure is not to resemble a maple leaf,
my other failures are operatic in comparison.

I've made too much of them,
too little of what might have calmed me down
enough to have integrity
enough to collaborate with the weather
and not to ask whether or how it's of use to me.

I understood these matters clearly
before I studied to be a fool.
Then horizon was nothing more than my skull
eighteen miles out there in my imagination
while I trampled civilizations underfoot.

Now I repent by examining this leaf.

Bones of ships and blue whales

Who was I not supposed to outlive?
I am awash in names. Sobs punctuate
my memory's writ like lonely buoys
sounding in the night. Who's to say
they would have used these years better?
Who's to judge how I have used them?
But once I found solar lanterns I knew
I hanker to shed light. I hang my poems
not in the most public places but where
I think they might do elementals good.
This is all I have ever understood
about prosody or all I have ever read.
I find the market wicked, the critics
occasionally a help, performance
punishment, reminiscence full of thorns.
I was not supposed to outlive any of them,
the ones who wash up in the moonlight
like bones of ships and blue whales.
Their names persist, not their touch,
nor glances we exchanged, and I distrust
few things more than names, so I patrol
barefoot at night studying
tides arguing with the disposition
of bones, pouring out of my skull
the glittering shards of the day
and imagining them as sea glass
collected by another boy.

As if furniture were galaxies

My vanishing point is within you.
I'm pointing to you over there.
How do I travel the distance
from here without disturbing
the disputed foreground?
Is it in dispute or are we
satisfied to be objects
denying our entanglement,
pretending to be sovereign
but locked in a pavane
across time and space as if
furniture were galaxies?

Lost scarves

Haunted, haunting (who is not a haunt?),
curtains murmuring in a blasted window,
intruders in the walls, smoky receptacles,
scurryings underfoot, mislabeled artifacts,
cupboard evidence of moments thrown away,
sorrows yellowing, shelf paper
of treasures treasured not as much
as what should happen next and never did so well.
Are we born haunted mansions,
boned creatures on a plain, abandoned stations,
ships heaved up from below, street lamps
looking like dandelion seeds to the myopic,
reminiscences of what we were, floating
like lost scarves in rogue squalls,
each other's ghosts who in their confusion
mistake themselves for objects?

Even if you have not noticed

Certain things you want to know are still there,
the rest can disappear along with you—
things no one would ever guess,
let them go free, don't say them here
or stay them there.
Words are green kindling, smoke.
It's time to act at vast distances
from the origins of your thoughts
so that everyone will know you will not be there
where they insist you ought to be,
and instead of second-guessing yourself
you will drop your data and depart.
All your personal and impersonal pronouns
have never been age-appropriate
or relevant,
but I have been fond even if you have not noticed.

Place

Summer pain

One of those mornings when nothing belongs in place,
especially not me, another item to be consumed.

A fresh wind promises nothing but whether
having to be weathered, not varnished,
morning for which we can't prepare
because dreams ill-fit us for illusions
where shadows escape their source,
voices flee the tongue and hide in the corners of the mouth,
sunlight is Van Gogh's brush maddening the ordinary,
wraithes molest irises, windows squirm, roots writhe,
lines crawl, buildings shrug, doors wink,
geometries set traps and we are frozen,
uncertain of the trigger, transfixed
by our predicament, enamored.

And under all the solemnity heaves a great belly laugh.

Morning, falsely glamored, is a politician.

We hear each other's beating hearts
and suffer hearing loss.

Who are we to think we know
when such mornings pounce
and we are prey?

Ruminant

Lonely places of great elegance
not yet gone to ruin,
trusting October's gold into gnarled November's hands.
I turn my collar up
and think of their inhabitants
now in their graves as my brothers and sisters.
Stone benches, red ivy, hushed fountain,
burlapped roses, and
the daylong rush of evening
ill-prepare me for the bloody windows
or the honk of taxis taking others
to airports and emergencies.
These are my urgencies
among cigarette butts and scuttling leaves.
I turn my collar up
and try to remember the proper collect
for the unutterably alone.

Breaking down in front of Butler Library

If torture's about not getting through
I don't think I've survived it.
I've gone with the torturer to live
in the shadows of a putrid alley.
What you see is a replicant
who thinks the Earth a stadium,
no one to care where he's gone
or who he was, and the torturer,
like all heroes, deaf, devoid
of those despised vestigial senses
that remind us of our daemonhood.
I remember those interrogations
from which I came out inside out,
how I was flown sack-headed
from Gitmo to the Port of Despair
dressed like other people to await
a filthy ship bound nowhere,
remember the terror of being born,
branded a terrorist for remembering,
for lack of a better name.
I saw too much in high relief,
became a suspect in the crib
for crimes against the state.
I couldn't filter the responses
to my colliding gaze.
They sickened me, I fell
down the marble stares before
the Butler Library of foreign gods

seasick with nostalgia for
a cradle in another room
rocked by a translucent hand.
Before such temples I bled out
and woke not needing blood.

A necessity of robots

Shapes and/or simulations
desperate not to disappear,
fragrances in a bottle,
whatever we are we're shaken
by gravity waves fine-tuning
our frequencies to stars,
and all our suppositions,
Taj Mahals and Louvres,
rest on watery foundations
subject to climate changes
so vast we invent robots
to understand them—
spare robots my memories,
I am incense swung at choirs,
fumes uncorked by children,
pixels letting go, shadows
passing over walls, flutter
in adjacent rooms, ghosts
undressing in a mirror,
both of us unblinking,
no longer trying to appear.

Hallowing

Gone to Japan and Peru
youth that shared its scent,
its eternal you
gone as winter's setting in.

We're more than our encounter
more than our loss,
but I am tired today
tired of what I can ever say.

We did not envy each other,
we may have wanted more
but in our curiosity
we leave a hallowed ground.

Charlie's Bar & Grille

Goodbye, salt shakers, drunks and lies,
   imperial bartenders, homefries—
     I have to take an eternal piss,
    relieve myself on a gravity wave.
You wouldn't talk to me of dandelions
    or misperceptions, so I'm going,
   but all of us who say we have to go,
     we never came, never came to
    in this bar & grille full of stiffs
we deposited with their various personalities,
yeah, never came in that sense of the word too,
   never became our own particular nova
    or much noticed other firmaments.
    Muddlers kept us busy, conversations
   we supposed were brilliant, vanities
we assigned to others. Under blinking neon
   the children we had been stared at us,
    wondering who we were. I'm going
     to do this wondering with them,
     to come to the mother senses
    I thought I had to check at the door.
     I may not make it to the back,
    to the filthy sink, the fungal bowl.
Charlie may step over me on his way to phone,
    and I doubt anybody will look up
  to the fulvous ceiling or even feel the draft
   a tin-winged shitbird makes leaving.

A Victorian wall

What is this welcome you've been looking for
in the twin jars of double U,
poured into and stirred, fired by belief?
A snow devil plays a brass trumpet in my head
when I ask, when I consider
where I've been, what I've done, who I'm asking.
I think it's a summons to join the polar bears
in their desperation on melting ice,
but it could be a pavane and I could be
a wraith who no longer has to watch its step.
My bones that misconvey embrace it for what it is
and feel no obligation to tell me,
me being an abstract painting skewed
on a Victorian wall.

Pushing a wheelbarrow in a bog

He picks up on more than he can handle,
more than he can explain
in the cyclotron of his brain
and in the vortex loses
his identity and resorts to ruses
to get through days that tilt
the world we've overbuilt
for money, days in which our eyes
fondle the uses of disguise.
So much was happening exactly when
there was so little time to distribute it
throughout the microbial empire of his being.
His senses were so heightened
he could not trust himself to bear it,
and he was liable to say
what anyone wanted least to hear
and scare himself in his mirror
by his propensity to disappear.
Pushing a wheelbarrow through a bog
is what it was like to lug his intuition around,
but he stuck wands of willow in the ground
and imagined lovers sitting under them,
and that he thought would do
for a semblance of decency,
not that anyone would notice,
nor that he wanted anyone to.

On the way to Syracuse

You be the lightning I'll be the mast,
together we'll enlighten the hull.
The amphorae will benefit
and the crew will hardly know,
they'll think good fortune struck
as Syracuse heaves into view, whereas
it was the ill fortune of the gods
and we, drenched in their piss,
happen to be their ground,
and so they bless us
for being there and bearing them
as if they had been cargo,
we their stewards not their slaves,
so busy with themselves
they'll hardly notice our afterglow.

Parley of queens

I'm dropping out of the sky
in disbelief that I assumed it habitat,
earth or ocean, certainly not the clouds
through which I pass,
certainly not the clouds I tear
and if I raise the question where
it's with the cunning of knowing
there's no time to answer it—
that's the kind of guile that's lent me lift
and while it's had its uses I regret it, plummeting.
No one's here to hear goodbye
and it would only be a screech
more like a Stuka than a hawk.
So, to use a figure of speech,
I'm used to the bottom falling out.
I always thought the right word
would rise from the sea like a water spout
and I'd ride it to a fabled place whose name
would be written on the private parts of queens
gathered to design another civilization
where light might stick and I'd crawl
under their table to sleep like a dog
woozy with their fragrances.

Boredom

What is erotic about boredom
is its untouchable contempt
for humble interests.
It eludes me, it belongs
to the otherwise engaged.
I am absorbed here between
raindrops and etceteras
of one foot in front of the other.
I don't know how to respond
to the sociable capable
of exquisite boredom
except to send emails
from the foreign places
of my chartless mind.

Otherland

Be here not there
where nothing is too small to hide behind

be here not there
where heaven reigneth down on earth too hard

be here not there
wherein there is contempt

Here in this otherland
where we are stranded

Shadowtime

Just

Can you think without words, see without light,
live without name body shape shadow
exist entirely beyond the limits of page
line sound meaning and yet love so mightily
all things passing through you
that you are the beatitude in whom I exist?

Who are you so incorporeal only sense
and scent betray your presence and words
must apologize for intruding? Please
don't answer my shameless question—let
it repent like sea glass in the tide.

I am just an apparition,
a shadow of something else.

Laundry

Everything has become remote except the laundry,
which can be sorted out and folded
until there is nothing left to do
but go to bed more humbly
than when I woke up
puffed up with light and determined
to make something of what happened,
to sort it out and fold it into
some kind of narrative
instead of letting it take off, a murder of ravens,
dotting an indeterminate sky
with parts of me in its beak.

I don't remember what I wrote
as well as what inspired it,
probably because I was sitting in some café
studying famous actors who were trying to be inconspicuous
and noticing they couldn't help but enjoy being noticed,
but I could help it better than I could help myself.
They were the lint that spoiled the laundry
because my eyes could filter them,
but I am afraid I have filtered my words all too well.
Nothing is more long ago than the last thing I wrote,
and that I call a benediction
because each word in its killer instinct,
trying to sum me up, is a shovelful full of dirt.

Mists

Did you ever save anyone's life?
Perhaps you did without knowing it,
like a dandelion between seams of cement.

No woman ever slipped me her number,
and I never thought myself grand enough
to slip anyone mine. But I had a few numbers,

if only because I liked to work them out,
never quite grasping that what might add up
did not necessarily mean it would work out.

I was good at guessing distances,
at hearing icebergs at night, and my compass
swung itself most elegantly when I ignored it.

I saved a few lives, but loomed
like shoals for others. I tried to warn
incautious ships away, even in obdurate mists.

Maddening me

I will not die of exhibitionism,
a small accomplishment
spoiled by writing about it.

May I be forgiven this
in the name of the lonely virtue
of having picked discard up?

To crave attention mightily…
not a criminal offense
but a scratched record of contempt.

A better man would feel sorry
when encountering it,
but in my ears its ill attunement maddens me.

Disturbances

If all treasures are cursed,
take care defining them,
consider where they rest,
how best to leave them there
and never say a word.
A poem is then a betrayal,
a painting a conspiracy,
fatal presumptions—
take your chances with them,
they celebrate less
than you can say about them,
and treasures say more
when asked forgiveness
for having been disturbed.

Ascent

The sky turned black and white
when I found the path to heaven.
White pines and dogwood lined
the sward. Dizziness of thyme
rose up with each step.
A sense of being watched
improbably reassured.
I cast no shadow and sang
a song I didn't know,
I became a dandelion seed.

A hill at Olana

All but human shadows remain—
will there be time to comprehend
what will comprehending do?—
perhaps we didn't need them,
perhaps we're already mad.
I'm walking up Church Hill, the sun behind me;
there will be no shadow to break my fall
when the valley tempts my feet.

Shadows

My shadow slips through the shadows of the trees
long and mournfully until the hawk stoops,
leaves scuttle, wind ripples the icy lake
and I take notice of the insignificance
of waiting for anything to happen
while it's where I misunderstood.

Pewter

I thought if I drank beer out of pewter
it would deliver me from the decisions I had made.
I thought the glass bottom would make clearer
what education had obscured.
The algorithm wasn't there, just the metallic taste
of so much gone wrong.
It was a long time ago. I was old.
Now the sob is gone.

The curvature of earth

No one dies properly,
too much is going on.
A pier is torn away,
firemen are marching,
and everyone wants
three dollars or
whatever you can spare.
We may have it backwards.
The old man in ICU
may be waking up
to a new life while
the newborn are dying
for all we know,
which is not very much.
What happened
to the ching-ching-ching
of cash registers
now that we sign our names
with our fingertips?
What happened to respect,
or was it a fantasy?
How can so much happen
while we notice so little?
Will anybody notice
me walking out the door,
mumbling to myself
in a gown, satisfied
to be a hologram,

passing through the trucks,
the ambulances, nodding
as if to fellow elementals,
trying heroically to make up
for all I didn't notice,
ignoring the curvature of earth
to stroll among the stars?

Vibrant irresolution

Vibrant irresolution, that's the stuff
of which, of which to hell with it,
Cubist innocence, Dadaderangement,
all in the interest of rescuing the child
locked in that unforgettable room,
curtains on fire, heart rattling the rafters,
snatching the child from parents' hands,
dirty, untrustworthy hands, all
in the interest of dying better
than being born, having been born,
there's a difference to be explored,
to make inquiries into the creases
and the folds of sordid narrative.
Yeah, that's the stuff to be considered
at 3 a.m. when dawn hesitates
to provide the shadows of another day.

As if Euclid and Pythagoras had not existed

This other shadow I knew better than to mention,
it obeys an alien law
as if Euclid and Pythagoras had not existed.
I pretended not to notice it to put off anyone who did,
but there were spasms in private parts
and amulets in crevasses of the mind
that called out to be used
like handguns and amphetamines.
That shadow darkened bright theaters,
it dragged down toggle switches like a deviant's hand.
If there was no light behind me
what was this darkening's source?
Not that it was like bad breath or speech impairment
but that it was allure
with which in decency you ought not truck.
And if I were to apologize for it what would the angel say?

Nailing afterimages to the wall

The time is always now
as a matter of respect
even when it's the death of you,
and yet each moment is
an afterimage of what we saw before,
afterlife relieving us
of the luggage of our names.
Let us now choose our shapes
with the substance of our dreams—
shadow and source,
particles of light, profligates of light, canticles of light,
above all, angels' flight
in the sidelong glance of strangers.
I'm done talking to you about this
until you give up trying to nail
afterimages to the wall.

Books by Djelloul Marbrook

Poetry

• *Far From Algiers* (2008, Kent State University Press, winner of the 2007 Stan and Tom Wick Poetry Prize and the 2010 International Book Award in Poetry)

• *Brushstrokes and Glances* (2010, Deerbrook Editions, Maine)

• *Brash Ice* (2014, Leaky Boot Press, UK)

• *Shadow of the Heron* (2016, Coda Crab Books, Seattle; out of print)

• *Riding Thermals to Winter Grounds* (2017, Leaky Boot Press, UK)

• *Air Tea with Dolores* (2017, Leaky Boot Press, UK)

• *Nothing True Has a Name* (2018, Leaky Boot Press, UK)

• *Even Now the Embers* (2018, Leaky Boot Press, UK)

• *Other Risks Include* (2018, Leaky Boot Press, UK)

• *The Seas Are Dolphins' Tears* (2018, Leaky Boot Press, UK)

• *Singing in the O of Not* (2019, Leaky Boot Press, UK)

• *The Loneliness of Shape* (2019, Leaky Boot Press, UK)

Fiction

• *Alice Miller's Room* (1999, OnlineOriginals.com, UK; reprinted as title story in *Making Room: Baltimore Stories*, 2017, Leaky Boot Press, UK)

• *Artemisia's Wolf* (2011, Prakash Books, India; reprinted as title story in *A Warding Circle: New York Stories*, 2017, Leaky Boot Press, UK)

• *Saraceno* (2012, Bliss Plot Press, NY)

- *Guest Boy* (2012, Mira Publishing House, UK; reprinted in 2018 in *Light Piercing Water* trilogy, Leaky Boot Press, UK)

- *Mean Bastards Making Nice* (2014, Leaky Boot Press, UK)

- *A Warding Circle: New York Stories* (2017, Leaky Boot Press, UK)